Herpetology

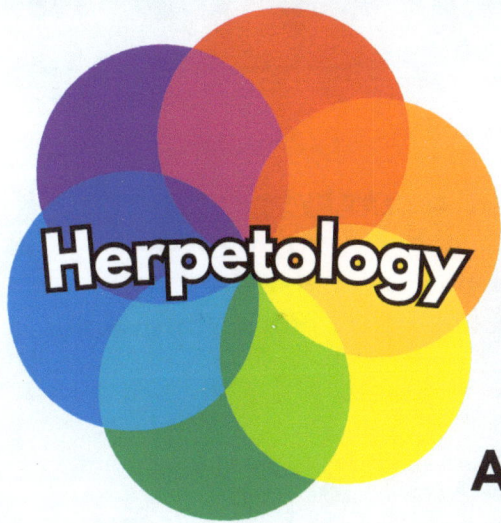

Book of COLORS

A Rainbow of Reptiles and Amphibians

AO PRESS

Jessica Lee Anderson

To Lori Gibson, Shawn Gray, and the whole fam—thanks for your friendship, support, and doing so much to spread herpetology love! - JLA

Photo credits, left to right, top to bottom: Front cover (Caiman lizard): Marshall Wayne; Interior cover: Life on White; Copyright page (Crested gecko): Bob_Eastman; Dedication page: David Kenny, eve_eve01genesis; p. 4: Nashepard, kikkerdirk, wildcatmad; p. 5: farinosa, Weber, Benjiecce; p. 6: komodo-adv, Vivera-a, nevenmn; p. 7: Alan Kelly, cavefish, David Kenny; p. 8: Robert Baker, Agus Fitriyanto, kikkerdirk; p. 9: lensblur, tunart, dangdumrong; p. 10: mjf795, eliechochron, Mesut Zengin; p. 11: Daniel Jara, Sane Noor, Markus Frenzel; p. 12: Azureus70, ArtisticOperations; p. 13: Reptiles4All, Maizal Chaniago; p. 14: David Kenny, Zoological Consult and Research VOF; p. 15: Tsepovia_Ekaterina, Kuchinta; p. 16: Weber, Ralfa Pandantya, cowboy 5437; p. 17: Aymeric Bein, izanbar; p. 18: Ken Griffiths, DKart, JAGTOR; p. 19: sk_img, by_ems; p. 20: Wirestock, Natalya Mamaeva, Zhivoderova; p. 21: Jessica Lee Anderson (thanks to Chris Janecek), digidreamgrafix; p. 22: Nathan Clifford, bookguy; p. 23: CreativeNature_nl, write-art_de; p. 24: Ken Griffiths, breckeni, William Sherman; p. 25: nynkevanholten, Ken Griffiths; p. 26: Andrew Helwich, Ken Griffiths, chubpydoopics; p. 27: georgewinstonlee, DPFishCo, Valmol48; p. 28: David Kenny (all); p. 29: Puwadol Jaturawutthichai, Songbird839; p. 30: easyart (both); p. 31: butterfuchs, Manakin; p. 32: tarikh, Nicholas Motto; p. 33: ePhotocorp, Kritsada Petchuay; p. 34: Michael Anderson; Back cover (Namib web-footed gecko): Alex Laske

This Book Belongs to:

_____

Herpetology is the study of reptiles and amphibians.

Poison dart frog

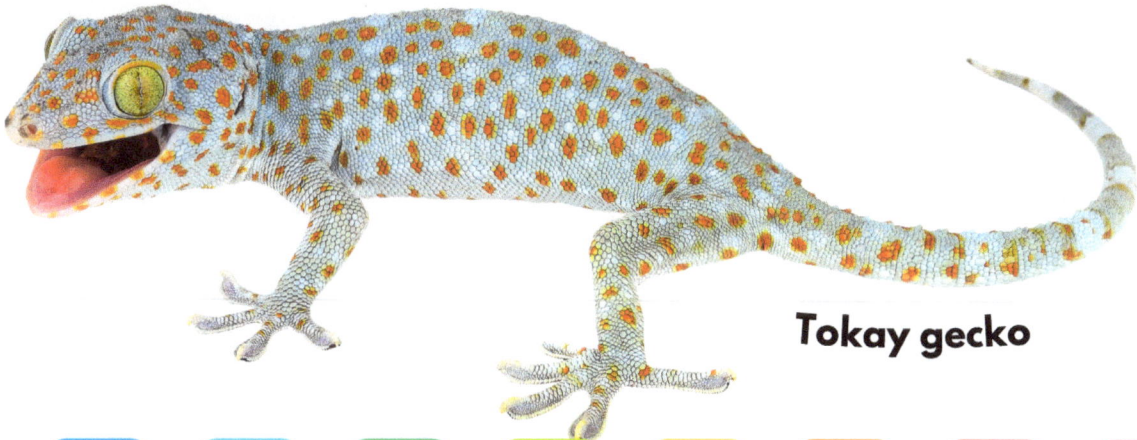

Tokay gecko

Red

Carolina pygmy rattlesnake

Strawberry poison dart frog

Reptiles like snakes and lizards have scales, but amphibians like frogs do not.

Red-spotted newt

Red

Madagascar tomato frog

Frogs and salamanders are amphibians. Amphibians can breathe air and absorb water through their skin.

Red salamander

Spiny-tailed lizard (Uromastyx)

Orange

Panther chameleon

Bearded dragon

Reptiles like bearded dragons and chameleons are types of lizards. Most lizards have long bodies and tails.

Oriental garden lizard

Orange

Eastern newt

Corn snake

Crested gecko

Many species of amphibians and reptiles are good climbers.

Yellow

Poison dart frog

White-lipped island pit viper

Some snake species have dangerous venom, and some frogs are poisonous if touched.

Eyelash viper

Yellow

Eastern box turtle

Bearded dragon

There are many different kinds of reptiles like snakes, lizards, and turtles.

Green

Green anole

Veiled chameleon

Some reptiles and amphibians like frogs, anoles, and chameleons eat things like insects.

Vietnamese flying tree frog

Green

Glass frog

Green tree python

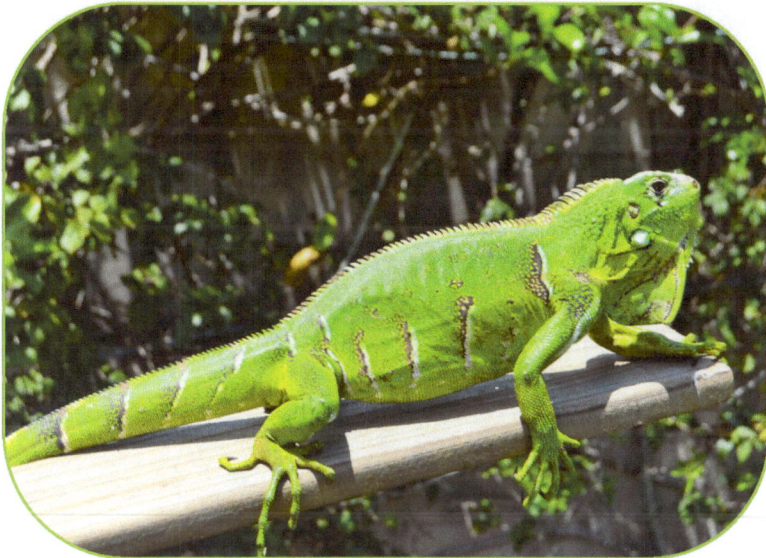

Green iguana

Reptiles and amphibians rely on the environment to regulate body temperature ("cold-blooded").

Blue

There are thousands of known reptiles and amphibians with new species still being discovered!

Blue poison dart frog

Blue iguana

Blue

Electric blue day gecko

Reptiles and amphibians can be found all over the world, except for Antarctica!

White-lipped island pit viper

Purple

Leopard gecko (lavender morph)

All reptiles and amphibians have bony skeletons.

Purple harlequin toad

Purple

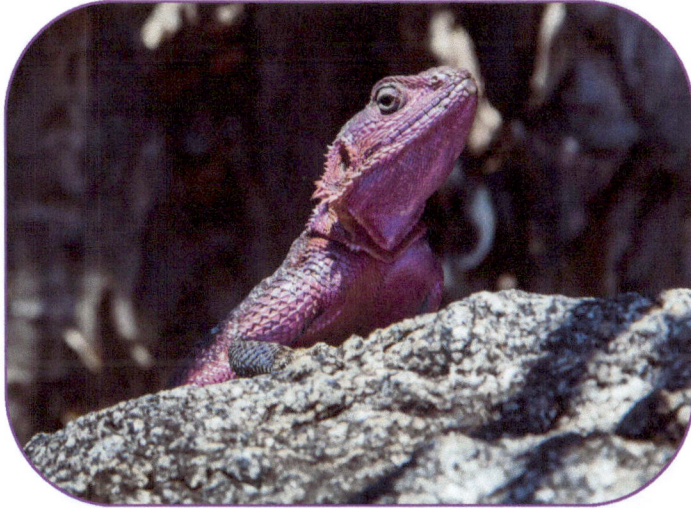

Mwanza flat-headed rock agama

Shapes and structures vary between species (and even within the same species)!

Mangrove pit viper

Pink

Florida worm lizard

Mangrove pit viper

Snakes don't have legs! Some lizard species don't have legs either.

Corn snake (amelanistic)

Pink

Panther chameleon

Most reptiles have tails, and some amphibians like salamanders do too.

Axolotls (Mexican salamanders)

Black

Black girdled lizard

Loggerhead sea turtle baby

Certain reptiles appear black due to a pigment called melanin that absorbs light.

Marine iguana

Black

Black pine snake

Caimans are related to alligators and have bony plates of armor called scutes.

Yacare caiman

White

Blue-eyed leucistic ball python

Leucistic leopard gecko

Certain reptiles can have a lack of pigment, making them appear white (leucistic).

Leucistic rat snake

White

Leucistic monocled cobra baby

Albinism in reptiles means a complete lack of melanin, making the eyes appear red, pink, or pale.

Albino alligator

Gray

Blue-tongued skink

Certain colors can help amphibians and reptiles blend into their environment (camouflage).

Gray tree frog

Gray

Monitor lizard

Tuatara

The tuatara is a type of reptile that is in a group all on its own!

Brown

Many-lined sun skink

Broadhead skink

Toads are a type of frog and skinks are a type of lizard.

Cane toad

Brown

Savannah monitor

Frilled lizard

Lizards can range in size and length, plus they can have different features (like a frill of skin around their neck).

Tan

Three-toed box turtle

Water-holding frog

Some reptiles and amphibians are tan— a pale, lighter version of brown.

King cobra

Tan

Side-blotched lizard

Horned toad

Sidewinder rattlesnake

Reptiles live in a variety of environments to include the harsh desert.

COLOR Combinations

Can you describe the colors and patterns of these frogs?

Poison dart frog

Fire-bellied toad

Poison dart frog

COLOR Combinations

Red-eared slider

Red-footed tortoise

What are some things you notice about the shapes, colors, and features of these two reptiles? Why do you think that matters?

COLOR Combinations

Mwanza flat-headed rock agama (Superman agama)

What are some colors and features you notice about these lizards? What do you think they do?

Fan-throated lizard

COLOR Combinations

Broadley's flat lizard

How are these reptiles similar and different when it comes to colors, shapes, and patterns?

San Francisco garter snakes

COLOR Combinations

Ornate day gecko

What are some similarities and differences you observe in the colors and features of these two lizards?

Eastern collared lizard

COLOR Combinations

Bombay shieldtail snake

Red-headed krait

What are the colors, shapes, and physical properties of these snakes? How are they the same or different?

Jessica Lee Anderson is an award-winning author of over 75 books for young readers including the NAOMI NASH chapter book series and many reptile books for young readers. Jessica loves spending time in nature and exploring the outdoors with her husband, Michael, and their daughter, Ava! Jessica loves finding colorful reptiles and amphibians near her home in Austin, Texas. You can learn more about Jessica by visiting www.jessicaleeanderson.com.

Check out these other books:

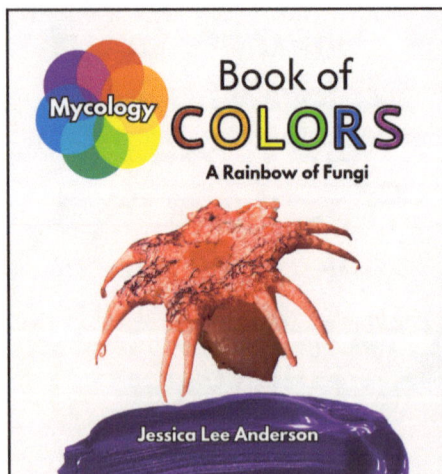

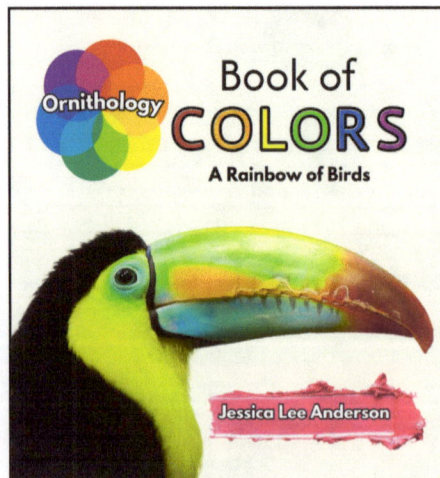

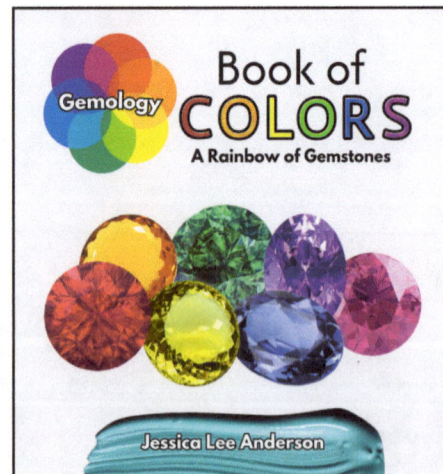

Mycology Book of COLORS
A Rainbow of Fungi
Jessica Lee Anderson

Ornithology Book of COLORS
A Rainbow of Birds
Jessica Lee Anderson

Gemology Book of COLORS
A Rainbow of Gemstones
Jessica Lee Anderson

www.ingramcontent.com/pod-product-compliance
Lightning Source LLC
Chambersburg PA
CBHW061144030426
42335CB00002B/100

* 9 7 8 1 9 6 4 0 7 8 2 3 6 *